The Quotation Bank

Power and Conflict

AQA Past and Present: Poetry Anthology

Copyright © 2019 Esse Publishing Limited

First published in 2019 by:
The Quotation Bank
Esse Publishing Limited

10 9 8 7 6 5 4 3 2 1

A CIP catalogue record for this book is available from the British Library.
ISBN 978-1-9999816-2-4

All enquiries to: contact@thequotationbank.co.uk

Printed and bound by Target Print Limited, Broad Lane, Cottenham, Cambridge CB24 8SW.

www.thequotationbank.co.uk

Introduction

What examiners are looking for 3

How The Quotation Bank can help you in your exams 4

How to use The Quotation Bank 4

The Poems

AQA Power and Conflict 5

Revision and Essay Planning

Major Themes 36

How to revise effectively 37

Sample essay, potential essay questions and revision activities 37

Glossary 41

Welcome to The Quotation Bank, the comprehensive guide to the poems and analysis you need to succeed in your exams.

Whilst you may have read the poems, understood the content and have a strong grasp of context, the majority of marks in the exam are for the ability to write a focused essay, full of quotations, and most importantly, quotations that you then analyse.

I think we all agree it is **analysis** that is the tricky part – and that is why we are here to help!

The Quotation Bank provides detailed material for each poem – we interpret the poems, analyse them, highlight literary techniques the poets have used, put them in context, and suggest which poems you might use in which essays.

At the end of **The Quotation Bank** we have put together a sample answer, essay plans and great revision exercises to help you prepare for your exam. We have also included a detailed glossary to make sure you completely understand what certain literary and poetical terms actually mean!

English Literature 9-1: What are examiners looking for?

24 of the 30 marks in the poetry question will be awarded for A01 and A02.

A01	Read, understand and respond to texts. Students should be able to: • Maintain a critical style and develop an *informed personal response* • Use textual references, *including quotations*, to support and illustrate *interpretations*.
A02	Analyse the *Language, Form and Structure* used by a writer to *create meanings and effects*, using *relevant subject terminology* where appropriate.

Basically, **AO1** is the ability to answer the question set, showing a good knowledge of the poems, and using quotations from the poems to back up ideas and interpretations.

AO2 is the ability to analyse these quotations, as well as the poetical techniques the writer uses, and to show you understand the effect of these on the reader.

We will also highlight elements of **AO3** – the context in which the poem is set.

How The Quotation Bank can help you in your exams.

The Quotation Bank is designed to make sure that every point you make in an essay clearly fulfils the Assessment Objectives an examiner will be using when marking your work.

Every poem comes with the following detailed material:

Interpretation: The interpretation of each poem allows you to fulfil **AO1**, responding to the text and giving an informed personal response.

Form and Structure: To move into the higher levels of the mark scheme it is important to analyse the effect of form and structure (**AO2**) as well as language and sentence level analysis.

Analysis: We have provided as much analysis (**AO2**) as possible. It is a great idea to analyse quotations in detail – you need to do more than just say what it means, but also what effect the language and poetical devices have on the reader.

Use in essays on… Your answer needs to be focused to fulfil **AO1**. This section helps you choose relevant poems and link them together for a stronger essay.

How to use The Quotation Bank.

Many students spend time learning poems by heart. Although there are some benefits to this, students often forget what they are meant to do with individual quotations once they get into the exam! Don't forget, the named poem in the exam will be printed on the exam paper.

By using **The Quotation Bank**, not only will you have a huge number of quotations to use in your essays, you will also have ideas on what to say about them, how to analyse them, how to link them together, and what questions to use them for.

Our detailed analysis covers a wide variety of different themes in each poem and can form the basis of your answer, making sure every point comes **directly from the poem (AO1)** and allowing you to **analyse language, form and structure (AO2)**. We also highlight where you can easily and effectively include **context (AO3)**.

The analysis in **The Quotation Bank** is excellent not only for revising the skills of **analysis (AO2)**, but also for helping you consider what poems could work well together for **comparison (AO1)**.

Ozymandias – Percy Bysshe Shelley

Interpretation: As a Pharaoh, Ozymandias elevates himself above all others. However, the supposed **"king of kings"** may rule over land, wealth and people, yet his power is futile against the strength of the ever-moving hands of time, and it is ironic that his power is outlived by the artwork that was created to immortalise him.

Form and Structure:

- The second-hand account of the statue (**"I met a traveller…who said"**) immediately lessens Ozymandias' power. He is no more than a story, and **"traveller"** implies he has become a tourist attraction, rather than something inspiring **"despair"**.
- The sonnet form has been utilised for hundreds of years, and Shelley's defined structure and unbroken use of iambic pentameter stress that both the sonnet and the statue, pieces of art, outlive the supposed power of Ozymandias.
- The first octave introduces the reader to the destruction of the statue and its pitiful state before introducing both its previous glory and Ozymandias himself. The volta at line 9 allows the sestet to convey the power and authority of Ozymandias, but by this point the reader already knows his power will fade.

Analysis:

- **"Antique"** could imply historical and cultural significance, or something of value and aesthetic appeal. However, it also suggests a fragile nature, as well as the implication it is a relic with little relevance in today's world. Indeed, further on in the poem the statue is nothing more than **"lifeless"**.
- **"Vast"** implies the strength and power of Ozymandias, reinforced by the solid associations of **"stone"**. However, the use of sibilance and enjambment links **"stone"** and **"stand"**, creating associations of immobility and passivity.
- The fact the **"legs"** are **"trunkless"** further accentuates Ozymandias' inadequacies.
- **"Half sunk"** not only creates an image of a statue that has been overwhelmed by the seemingly harmless **"sand"**, **"half"** also suggests the statue is desperately, but unsuccessfully, trying to survive.
- The brief pauses after **"half sunk"** and **"a shattered visage lies"** both cause the reader to dwell on the destruction of the statue before we are introduced to Ozymandias.
- **"Shattered"** implies the visage is irreparably damaged, never to be returned to its previously intimidating state, whilst **"lies"** further accentuates its passivity.
- The images of **"frown"**, **"wrinkled lip"** and **"sneer"** all create a tone of contempt, with the polysyndeton lengthening

the feeling of disdain created.

- This contempt is made threatening with the use of **"cold command"**. **"Command"** implies the power he holds, and **"cold"** suggests he wields it dispassionately. Furthermore, the harsh alliteration of the "c" sound accentuates the menacing tone behind his **"command"**.
- **"Cold"** is juxtaposed with **"passions"** – whilst **"frown"**, **"wrinkled"** and **"sneer"** seem unpleasant, the hatred behind them is intensified by the **"passions"** that caused them in the first place.
- The brief pause after **"survive"** creates an ominous image of Ozymandias' negative qualities resiliently fighting on, whilst **"stamped"** implies both aggression and permanence.
- **"The hand that mocked"** could be interpreted in several ways, but many interpretations depict the power the sculptor has over Ozymandias. On the one hand, **"mocked"** could suggest the sculptor has the power to ridicule and humiliate Ozymandias by producing a sculpture that accentuates his negative features.
- Alternatively, **"mocked"** could reference the hand that created the sculpture; for all of Ozymandias' power, he is reliant on an artist to preserve his legacy, again allowing Shelley to stress the power of artistic expression.
- The image of a **"pedestal"** is ironic – designed to elevate Ozymandias above his people, it now contains nothing but empty **"words"**.
- The arrogant claim to be **"king of kings"** is made all the more hubristic by his reference to other kings as **"ye Mighty"**, giving them an almost spiritual significance, and yet he still uses the imperatives **"look"** and **"despair"**.
- The single clause sentence **"Nothing beside remains"** emphatically presents the fact that Ozymandias' power is now **"Nothing"** – he has been reduced to **"decay"**, implying a continuous rotting, and a **"colossal wreck"**, suggesting he has been destroyed beyond repair.
- The structure of the poem means Ozymandias' words seem strong and powerful, but they are then immediately undermined and defined as **"Nothing"**.
- The true power in the poem lies in the natural world. The harsh, plosive "b" creates an aggressive sound, accentuating the intimidatingly endless association of **"boundless"** and the vast emptiness of **"bare"**.
- This endless, barren wasteland is reinforced by **"lone and level"**, with the sibilance of **"sands stretch"** elongating the phrase and mimicking the scale of the desert that is conveyed by the phrase **"far away"**.

Use in essays on…Nature; Human Control; Identity; Time; Weakness

London – William Blake

Interpretation: London was one of the most powerful and influential cities in the world when 'London' was published – however, Blake depicts a city that also suffers immensely with conflict and corruption, be it religious hypocrisy, political abuse or human suffering, on both a mental and physical level.

Form and Structure:
- The first-person narrative gives validity to the message of the poem. The poem conveys the real-life observations of someone who is actively and observantly wandering through **"each chartered street"**, paying far more attention to the human suffering on show than any institution ever does.
- The ABAB rhyme scheme is relentless, creating a sense of the incessant suffering within the city, and a tone of weariness and depression is accentuated by the rhyme of the deep, heavy vowel sounds. The rhythm of the lines mimics the narrator's journey, trudging through London, burdened by suffering.
- The first two stanzas deal with human misery and are highly sensual in nature; specific examples are seen, heard and felt. Blake explores the institutions at fault for this suffering in the third stanza, before returning to focus on the victims of the suffering in the final stanza.

Analysis:
- The poem begins with a sense of purposelessness and futility. **"Wander"** does not imply a pleasant stroll, but rather a desperate, aimless walk through the city.
- The repetition of **"chartered"** highlights the power institutions hold; whilst a **"street"** may be legitimately **"chartered"** (under legal control), the **"Thames"** is a powerful natural force, symbolic of London's greatness.
- A **"chartered Thames"** depicts mankind controlling nature for its own gain, emphasised by the juxtaposition between the freedom of **"flow"** and the restrictive **"chartered"**.
- Repetition of **"marks"** has associations with scars and injury, accentuated by the alliteration of **"weakness"** (implying physical harm) and **"woe"** (conveying mental suffering).
- They are on **"every man"** and **"every infant['s]"**, and are both external (**"every face"**) and internal (**"every voice"**) in nature.

- **"Infant's"** should be an image of purity and innocence, yet the abstract noun **"fear"** implies they are already aware of the dangers and threats in the world.
- Repetition of **"cry"** links the infant to the chimney-sweeper and images of helpless, exploited children, suggesting their **"fear"** does not decrease as they get older.
- **"Manacles"** are a cruel image of physical restraint and suffering that are utilised by corrupt entities, with **"forged"** stressing their strength. Yet these are **"mind-forged"**, implying an even greater control over an individual, as they control both the body and soul.
- A **"church"** should symbolise spiritual salvation and sanctuary, yet **"black'ning"** conveys a corruption within the powerful Church establishment.
- Furthermore, **"palace walls"** should represent strength and security within a city, providing protection to its citizens; however, a **"soldier"**, an image of supposed power and might, is **"hapless"**, with his **"sigh"** conveying his lack of strength or purpose. The sibilant **"soldier's sigh"** does not sound powerful and dynamic, but rather cumbersome and weary.
- The third stanza concludes with examples of human cries, **"weakness"** and **"woe"** culminating in a comprehensive physical destruction which **"runs in blood down palace walls"** – it is ironic that the Thames is **"chartered"** but the blood flows freely.
- London is a vibrant city, yet **"midnight"** implies darkness and danger, reinforced when the narrator states that all **"I hear"** at this time is **"youthful harlot[']s"** and **"new-born infants"**.
- The final stanza highlights how the abuse of power by powerful institutions destroys innocence - **"harlot's"** implies sexual sin, and **"curse"** combines both offensive language and a witch's evil spell, yet this **"curse"** comes from someone **"youthful"**.
- Furthermore, rather than be protected and kept safe, the **"new-born infant"** suffers the violence of **"blasts"** and is reduced to a **"tear"**.
- **"Marriage"** should be a loving, spiritual connection between two people. Instead, it is now connected with death (**"hearse"**), bought on by **"plagues"**, which suggest disease.
- The juxtaposition of **"marriage hearse"** is a disturbingly conflicted image to end the poem.

Use in essays on…Individuals vs Society; Misuse of Power; Religion; Oppression; Fear; Weakness

Extract from The Prelude – William Wordsworth

Interpretation: Wordsworth depicts a pivotal change in the boy's life. Seeing nature as docile and controllable, an experience with the sublime power of nature leaves him confused and troubled, no longer able to return to the innocence he once held.

Form and Structure:
- The first-person narrative tracks the boy's development. Blank verse and iambic pentameter in the first section create a calm, carefree tone. By the end of the poem the verse and rhythm are frequently interrupted with caesura, mimicking the fractured, troubled state of the boy's mind.
- After the calmness of the first sentence, **"straight"**, **"stepping"** and **"pushed"** have active, dynamic connotations. **"I unloosed her chain"** is a metaphor for the child breaking free of home and beginning to seek new adventures.
- The volta in line 11 **("But now")** shifts the tone from childish to adult emotions. The deliberate pause after **"swan"** highlights another shift in tone and focus – the narrator has grown in confidence, so nature decides to take back control.
- The narrator's fear is emphasised by the frantic rhythm of **"I struck and struck again"**, an entirely futile action since the sibilance in **"growing still in stature"** emphasises the continual presence and threat of nature.
- Upon his return, everything has changed. The **"willow"** and the **"rocky cove"** are **"covert"**, implying a place of secrecy. The **"little boat"** is now a functional **"bark"** with the tender **"home"** replaced with the coldness of **"mooring-place"**.

Analysis:
- The relaxing image of **"summer evening"** is peaceful, and **"a little boat"** is perfect for childish play; later it matures into an **"elfin pinnace"**, with **"elfin"** implying he has been seduced by something supernatural, and **"pinnace"** having associations with commerce or warfare. The boat's **"usual home"** implies safety and security within the **"rocky cove"**.
- An **"act of stealth"** implies the child knew what he was doing was wrong; the oxymoronic **"troubled pleasure"** moves the child from a world of innocence to a place where **"pleasure"** confuses the boundaries between right and wrong.
- The beauty (**"moon"** and **"light"**), magic (**"glittering"** and **"sparkling"**) and peace (**"small circles"** and **"idly"**) of childhood have gone. **"Leaving behind"** implies a rejection of youth, but **"melted"** hides **"darkness"** that is coming.
- **"Like one who rows"** suggests a lack of physical maturity; he is **"like one"**, but not yet ready. Pride emerges alongside determination in the **"unswerving line"**, **"chosen point"** and **"fixed my view"**. The ambitious aim of the **"summit"**, not just of the **"horizon"** but of its **"utmost boundary"**, implies a determination for the most extreme adventure.
- **"Led by her"** in line 1 depicts nature as a guide. Aggressive vowel sounds in **"craggy"** and the perilous associations of

- **"ridge"** stress a different side to nature. The narrator aims **"far above"** for **"the stars"**, yet this new world has a drab **"grey sky"**, not the idyllic **"summer evening"** of earlier.
- The transition to manhood is tentative, with **"dipped"** implying caution, yet his transition gains pace. **"Stroke"** is strong, with **"rose"** symbolising his growth in stature, and **"my oars into the silent lake"** begin to control and dominate nature.
- The adverb **"lustily"** alongside **"heaving"** has sexual connotations, implying a sexual awakening. The simile **"like a swan"** depicts the power and grace of his boat, but in this context **"swan"** could allude to the myth of 'Leda and the Swan'. Zeus, disguised as a swan, seduces Leda for his own **"troubled pleasure"**.
- The power of nature is emphasised by the simple **"huge peak, black and huge"**. **"Peak"** is nature at its grandest, whilst **"black"** is far more intimidating than the **"grey sky"**. **"Huge"** lacks beauty and is instead imposing and threatening.
- The personification of the mountain enhances its threat. **"Voluntary power"** and **"instinct"** depict it as a great hunter, reinforced by **"upreared its head"**. The boy's immaturity does not allow him to identify the threat. The vague **"grim shape"** and lack of understanding in **"so it seemed"** depicts his naivety. **"Towered up"** reinforces the imposing presence of nature. Being **"between me and the stars"** depicts nature standing in the way of any heavenly salvation.
- The sibilant **"still,/For so it seemed"**, and the alliteration of **"measured motion"** and **"like a living"** mimics the speed with which the mountain **"strode after me"**. **"Strode"** and **"measured motion"**, alongside the associations of **"purpose"**, create an image of the boy being deliberately hunted. **"My oars"** were once carefully **"dipped"**; now they are **"trembling"**, and the **"silent lake"**, something safe and contained by boundaries, is now the endless **"silent water"**.
- The previous **"act of stealth"** had associations with adventure and exploration, not wrongdoing – now he has been defeated he simply **"stole my way/Back"**. **"Grave"** and **"serious"** convey the burdened mindset of the adult world, whilst **"spectacle"** conveys the impression nature has made on the boy, enhanced by its duration over **"many days"**.
- **"Familiar shapes"** provided comfort; **"pleasant images"**, the sibilant **"sea or sky"** and vibrant **"colours of green"** suggest a pleasing bond with nature. The repetition of **"no"** emphatically rejects this past relationship – it is gone forever.
- **"Dim"**, **"undetermined"** and **"unknown"** convey confusion, with **"modes of being"** reducing life to a perfunctory status. **"Darkness"** and **"blank"** imply an emptiness to life, with **"solitude"** and **"desertion"** stressing his isolation.
- **"Do not live/Like living men"** conveys his inability to articulate the natural world around him, with **"huge and mighty forms"** reinforcing nature's power. Childish daydreams have been corrupted as nature **"moved slowly"**, preserving a haunting presence in **"my dreams"**; **"troubled pleasure"** at the start of the poem is now simply **"trouble"**.

Use in essays on…Weakness; Nature; Fear; Futility; Identity; Human Control

My Last Duchess – Robert Browning

Interpretation: The Duke is the embodiment of power and control. He controls who lives and dies simply by giving **"commands"**; he picks and chooses wives based on the strength of his **"nine-hundred-years-old name"**; and be it Counts, suitors or artists, everyone will **"sit"** or **"rise"** as he sees fit.

Form and Structure:

- The poem's structure conveys aspects of the Duke's controlling nature. Whilst two people are present, the poem's form is a monologue. The Duke controls the conversation, silencing the visitor entirely. Repetition of **"Sir"** creates a pleasant, formal tone that disguises the threatening content of the poem.
- The Duke asks questions throughout the poem, but they are all rhetorical in nature – they are to emphasise his control over his guest, not to elicit a response. This is reinforced by the fact the Duke answers a number of his own questions.
- Rhyming couplets convey the Duke as controlled, calm and eloquent, and the mixture of enjambment and caesura often creates a conversational tone; the Duke utilises these techniques to convey a welcoming demeanour. However, between lines 31-45, pauses and fractured sentences mimic the lack of control in his mind, accentuating his increasing anger.

Analysis:

- The possessive **"my"** immediately introduces a sense of control and ownership. His wife is referred to as **"Duchess"** (defined by marriage), **"she"** (lacking identity) and **"piece"** (defining her as an object). Later she becomes nothing more than a **"pictured countenance"** and **"such an one"**. The Duke has God-like qualities – he can make the Duchess seem **"alive"**, and even controls who views her **("since none puts by/ The curtain I have drawn for you, but I")**.
- **"Will't please you"** seems polite, but the Duke's threatening character is reinforced by the imperative **"sit and look at her"** – he does not let the listener stand until line 47 **("will't please you rise")**. People only speak to him **"if they durst"** – the narrative serves as a warning if he does not get **"my object"**. The Duke's pride is heightened by the deliberate naming of **"Fra Pandolf"** and **"Claus of Innsbruck"**. He validates himself by employing artists to work for him.
- The Duke's delusional nature is stressed by the fact people **"seemed"** to **"ask me"**, and by his statement that **"not the first/Are you to turn and ask"**; in fact, **"seemed"** stresses no one ever asked about the Duchess – it is all in his mind.
- Their relationship was clearly a distant one. **"Her husband's presence"** lacks intimacy and human contact, and later **"I passed her"** is devoid of all physical or verbal contact. **"Spot/Of joy"**, **"faint/Half-flush"** and **"blush"** are sensual images that suggest a flirtatious side to the Duchess. She is excited by Fra Pandolf's **"courtesy"**, but the disdain from the

- sibilant **"such stuff"** and derogatory **"stuff"** implies the Duke had no desire to engage in such behaviour with his wife.
- The tenderness of Fra Pandolf's statements become threatening through the violent imagery of **"dies along her throat"**.
- **"Enough"**, **"too soon"**, **"too easily"** and **"whate'er"** suggest the Duchess lacks an appreciation of social hierarchy. She sees value **"everywhere"**, and the anger in the monosyllabic **"Sir, 'twas all one"** conveys the Duke's resentment.
- The alliterative **"dropping of the daylight"** has a romantic tone, and **"bough of cherries"**, **"orchard"** and **"white mule"** are idealised images, yet the juxtaposition of **"my favour"** with the contempt felt in **"officious fool"** implies the Duke feels **"all and each"** are certainly not all **"alike"** – he sits at the top of the hierarchy.
- **"My gift"** is thoughtful yet **"ranked"** suggests it was given to assert power. The compound word **"nine-hundred-years-old name"** is esteemed by the Duke, but to the Duchess it is no more than **"anybody's gift"**. **"Trifling"** debases the Duke's name, reinforced by the repetition of **"stoop"**, further alluding to a literal lowering of his status. His false humility in claiming **"I have not"** the **"skill/In speech"** is then followed with a list of controlling, manipulative statements.
- In **"make your will/Quite clear"** the stress falls on **"quite"**, conveying his precise expectations, increased by the exact requirements of **"the mark"**. Furthermore, **"disgusts me"** seems disproportionate to the seemingly innocent **"Just this /Or that"**, and alongside **"miss"** and **"exceed"**, it is clear the Duchess could never meet the Duke's exacting standards.
- The contrast between **"let/Herself be lessoned"** and **"made excuse"** confirms the Duchess has two options; both end in her death. A caesura before **"and I choose/Never to stoop"** emphasises this threatening, defiant statement.
- The angry tone of **"This grew"** highlights the problem is with the Duke, not the Duchess. **"This"** refers to the Duchess' frequent smiles, not anything more sinister. Short clauses after the **"smile"** creates an ominous tone – threatening connotations of **"I gave commands"** sound like military orders, and the sibilant **"smiles stopped"** accentuate his sinister behaviour. The juxtaposition between **"smiles"** and the controlling **"stopped"** confirms his misuse of power.
- The quest for wealth, not love, is evident in **"munificence"**, **"ample"** and **"dowry"** – the business-like nature of the transaction is juxtaposed with the human qualities of **"fair daughter's self"**, with **"fair"** suggesting her innocence and vulnerability, and **"self"** stressing he aims to take over her identity.
- Subtle suggestions of control continue. **"Nay"** implies the visitor tries to leave, but the Duke insists **"we'll go/Together down"**. Intimidation is further present in the harsh alliteration of **"Notice Neptune"**, alongside the imperative **"Notice"** and reference to mighty **"Neptune"**, reinforcing the Duke's aggressive nature. **"Taming a sea-horse"** ends the poem on the image of a God ruthlessly controlling a vulnerable subject – a metaphor for the Duke himself.

Use in essays on…Human Control; Misuse of Power; Appearance vs Reality; Family Conflict

The Charge of the Light Brigade – Alfred Lord Tennyson

Interpretation: Focus is often placed on who was to blame for the failed assault that inspired Tennyson's 'The Charge of the Light Brigade'; the assault was chaotic, deadly and futile. However, Tennyson focuses on the brave soldiers and the heroic actions of those Cavalrymen who served their country with honour, nobility and glory.

Form and Structure:

- The narrative's chronological structure builds tension as each stanza develops; the reader is aware of the battle's outcome, increasing sympathy for the soldiers and anger at those who **"blunder'd"**. The final stanza directly addresses the reader; it is short and emphatic, full of imperatives and exclamations, demanding we **"honour"** the **"noble six hundred!"**
- The longer fourth stanza focuses on the heroic action of the soldiers; it depicts the bravery of the soldiers, but for the first time the refrain **"Rode the six hundred"** has become **"Not the six hundred"**, stressing the sacrifice they made.
- The rhyme scheme varies, at times using rhyming couplets or triplets, or using half-rhymes, to mimic the chaos of battle. For example, in stanza 2 the soldiers cannot hesitate – they hurtle into battle unquestioningly, with the use of **"reply"**, **"why"** and **"die"** stressing the rapid nature of their demise.

Analysis:

- Repetition of **"half a league"** creates a strong rhythm, mimicking soldiers and horses galloping into battle. **"Onward"**, **"rode"**, **"forward"** and **"charge"** are dynamic, emphasising the soldier's movement, never hesitating or looking back.
- Repetition of **"valley of Death"** is a biblical allusion, giving their actions spiritual significance. However, the **"valley of Death"** could be seen as an image of hell on earth, reinforced later when the valley is depicted as the **"mouth of Hell"**.
- War creates anonymity. **"The six hundred"** are simply another weapon **"some one"** gets to use indiscriminately, and **"'Charge for the guns!' he said"** stresses the insanity of war (charging at guns armed only with a sword).
- **"He said"** depicts a nameless authority; no one takes responsibility. The incompetency of the authorities is highlighted by the fact **"the soldier knew"** it was wrong, with **"blunder'd"** again understating the human suffering caused.
- Repetition of **"theirs"** confirms it is they who have to act on this blunder, yet the inclusion of **"not to"** implies they are powerless to question **("make reply")** or seek clarification **("reason why")**. **"But to"** stresses they only have one option.
- **"Do and die"** uses the alliterative 'd' to create a heroic tone, but **"<u>and</u> die"** rather than '<u>or</u> die' confirms that after they **"do"**, **"die"** is the only outcome. Repetition of **"cannon"** mimics the barrage of the guns; **"right"**, **"left"**, **"in front"** and in stanza 5, **"behind"**, create an image of entrapment. There is no escaping the **"jaws of Death"**. Aggressive consonants

in **"Volley'd"**, **"thunder'd"** and **"storm'd"** reinforce the violent **"cannon"** and amplify the onslaught of violence.

- **"Thunder'd"** and **"storm'd"** have powerful natural connotations, as if the earth itself has turned on them. It could even elevate the onslaught to a god-like level, as if the gods themselves were raining down storms and thunder upon them.
- Harsh sibilance in **"shot and shell"**, as well as the precision of **"shot"** in contrast to the indiscriminate **"shell"**, accentuates the all-encompassing attack on them. Structurally, the fact **"Volley'd and thunder'd;/Storm'd at with shot and shell"** is repeated in stanza 5 emphasises the lengthy duration the soldiers suffered for.
- The adverb **"boldly"** implies bravery, **"they rode"** their active involvement, and **"well"** the skill with which they fought. However, the personification of **"Death"** and **"Hell"** (two depictions of evil), as well as reference to **"jaws"** and **"mouth"**, creates an image of soldiers as nothing more than prey waiting to be consumed.
- The soldiers are skilful troops. Repetition of **"Flash'd"** implies precision, and the sibilant **"sabre-stroke"** mimics clinical swordsmanship. **"Stroke"** is subtle and deliberate, unlike the mass destruction of **"cannon"**. **"Sabres"** are no match for **"cannon"**, **"shot and shell"**, yet **"Sabring the gunners"** elevates the cavalry above the indiscriminate **"gunners"**.
- **"Charging"** and **"Plunged"** have powerful associations, particularly in the face of **"an army"** and **"battery-smoke"**.
- The fact the enemy **"Reel'd"** (implying disorientation), **"Shatter'd"** (suggesting destroyed) and **"sunder'd"** (depicting it as torn apart) should result in a great military victory. However, **"but"** foreshadows the negative outcome, and the repetition of **"not/Not"** places great focus on the loss suffered. This loss is more painful as **"All the world wonder'd"**. **"All"** implies defeat was obvious to even the most naïve observer – the alliterative **"world wonder'd"** stresses the fact the **"world"** could predict it would end tragically, and **"wonder'd"** conveys their sense of helplessness and disbelief.
- The alliterative **"horse and hero"** depicts an effective combat unit, with **"so well"** asserting the soldiers' skill, but the litotes of **"fell"** minimises their horrific deaths. Whilst **"came thro'"** and **"Back from"** suggests an escape from death, **"All that was left"** is an image of a decimated **"Light Brigade"**, with the repetition of **"left"** emphasising the loss.
- The rhetorical question **"When can their glory fade?"** is answered by the creation of the poem itself – it is a monument to their bravery. **"O"** is a personal, human response from the narrator – he is overwhelmed by their actions. **"Wild"** may imply animalistic and uncontrolled behaviour, but it also praises the instinctive, unquestioning patriotism they displayed.
- The replacement of **"the six hundred"** with **"Noble six hundred!"** emphasises the core message of the poem; what they did was **"noble"**, never to be forgotten.

Use in essays on…War; Misuse of Power; Fear; Futility; Identity

Exposure – Wilfred Owen

Interpretation: In war, threats of enemies, weapons and battles are common dangers a soldier will face. Yet, whilst in the midst of conflict, Owen articulates the notion that the most ominous threat is that posed by nature, and whilst physical suffering is frequent, so too is the mental turmoil that a soldier must endure.

Form and Structure:
- Generally following an ABBAC rhyme scheme, the use of imperfect rhyme is jarring and uncomfortable, much like the soldier's movement. **"Knive us"/"nervous"**, and **"silent"/"salient"** create an awkward tone that lacks fluency.
- This is reinforced by Owen's sentence structure. Varied and inconsistent use of caesura, ellipsis and enjambment create a lack of regularity and control, perfectly mimicking the environment the soldiers are in.
- However, each of the stanzas is of equal length, with the same sentence pattern, creating a monotonous, repetitive atmosphere throughout the poem.
- The final line of each stanza confirms the futility of war **("But nothing happens")**, the confusion (**"what are we doing here?"** and **"Is it that we are dying?"**), the rejection of life (**"we turn back to our dying"**), and even of God himself (**"For love of God seems dying"**).

Analysis:
- **"Ache"** is a physical, sensual word, yet **"our brains ache"** implies mental suffering is more prominent than the physical. Mental disintegration continues – **"confuse"** stresses their lack of understanding, and **"our memory"** highlights the confusion about their past as well as uncertainty about the future.
- Weapons themselves seem somewhat ineffectual. **"Low, drooping flares"** lack menace; the **"gunnery rumbles"** but **"flickering"** lacks real threat, and **"incessantly"** suggests the continual noise, rather than being shelled, is the real fear.
- When **"bullets streak the silence"** they are **"less deadly than the air"**. The juxtaposition between solid **"bullets"** and harmless **"air"** emphasises the real threat to soldiers. In war, the natural world is a greater danger than the enemy. Owen personifies nature to convey the active part it plays in their suffering.
- **"Winds"** are **"iced"**, implying physical discomfort but also a cold, emotionless attack, with **"merciless"** reinforcing the unfeeling and relentless assault, and **"knive us"** adding a frenzied nature to it. In the second stanza winds become **"mad gusts"**; **"mad"** implies the insanity of war is so intense it even corrupts nature.

- By stanza 3, even the cycle of night and day has been corrupted. **"Dawn"** should signal a fresh new day; instead it brings **"misery"** and is personified as an enemy. The repetition of the 'm' sound reinforces dawn's army is both vast (**"massing"**) and depressing (**"melancholy"**) as well as relentless (**"attacks once more"**).
- The misery dawn brings is endless (**"war lasts"**), overwhelming (**"rain soaks"**) and hangs over the soldiers in a threatening, burdensome manner (**"clouds sag stormy"**). The sibilant 's' further accentuates the heavy, weary tone.
- Dawn's corruption is matched by the snow. Usually a romanticised image of winter, the oxymoronic **"black with snow"** is a vivid image of natural corruption. The snow turns the **"air"**, usually pure and life-giving, into something **"deadly"**.
- Nature's character is malignant; the fricative 'f' and associations of **"flowing flakes"** alongside **"sidelong"** create a sense of the deliberate, incessant attack.
- The tri-colon **"flock"** (suggesting **"flakes"** ambushing the soldiers as a cohesive unit), **"pause"** (implying a strategic regrouping) and **"renew"** (conveying a re-invigorated battle charge) further accentuates nature's malicious attacks.
- The wind simply watches with **"nonchalance"**; it has no concern for humanity.
- In the fifth stanza, **"stealth"** implies the snow attacks with well-drilled precision, and the fricative 'f' in the first line elongates the sense of the suffering the soldiers endure. **"Fingering"** and **"feeling"** implies a deliberate physical assault, with **"our faces"** reminding the reader of the humanity of the victim.
- The soldiers remain passive as nature overwhelms them. Rather than fight to survive, they **"cringe"**, **"stare"** and **"drowse"**, entirely futile actions. Indeed, nature has rendered the soldiers useless – **"snow-dazed"** conveys mental disintegration, and **"sun-dozed"** reinforces the physical lethargy.
- All memory of **"dreams"** are now **"forgotten"** and they are entirely defeated.
- Finally, it is not the enemy that defeats the soldiers, but the environment. **"Frost will fasten"** creates an image of soldiers buried beneath the snowfall; it will **"fasten on this mud and us"** which reduces humanity to the same level as dirt.
- War corrupts all aspects of life. **"Silent"** and **"night"** should provide peace and rest, particularly when **"wearied"**. However, they **"keep awake"**, and **"because"** stresses that a silent night brings fear, not respite. **"Silence"** has associations of peacefulness, but it has become corrupted and causes soldiers to be **"worried"**.
- **"Sentries"** evokes strength and safety, but **"worried"** and the tri-colon **"whisper, curious, nervous"** conveys fear and tension that infiltrates even the bravest man.
- Both **"watching"** and **"we hear"** are passive actions, reinforced later as soldiers die in a snowstorm; **"we watch them**

wandering" is passive in the face of death, the alliterative 'w' creating a tone of resignation before the inevitable occurs.
- Images of **"wire"** and **"brambles"** imply weapons of war are so ingrained in the earth, they have become almost natural, like **"brambles"**. Whilst the brutal associations of **"agonies of men"** is deeply human, the verb **"twitching"** depicts soldiers as nothing more than insects, like prey caught in a web. The futility of war is stressed by **"far off"**, **"dull rumour"** and **"some other war"**. They have no real impact on the war, and heroic patriotism is a distant memory.
- War removes identity. The repetition of the first-person plural **"our"**, **"we"** and **"us"** may depict a collective unit, but it destroys individuality, later evident in **"shivering ranks of grey"**, unidentifiable and devoid of colour or personality.
- By the end of the poem they are simply **"faces"**, worthy of nothing more than a **"pause"**, with **"half-known"** implying the unfulfilled nature of their short lives.
- Suffering grows as the natural world continues as usual. **"Grassier ditches"** become trenches, but for the **"blackbird"** they are **"littered with blossoms"**, juxtaposing human horrors; **"fusses"** implies the bird has little to worry about.
- Memories of home increase the suffering. **"Ghosts"** implies soldiers are already resigned to death. Rather than being released freely into the afterlife, **"slowly"** alongside **"drag"** implies even in death they are burdened and weary, reinforced by the elongated 'o' sound in **"slowly"**, **"ghosts"** and **"home"**.
- The **"sunk fires"** radiate heat in contrast to **"frost"**, with **"jewels"** implying how precious the heat is, and **"dark-red"** stressing the vibrant colour of life away from war, as opposed to the **"black"** and **"grey"** of the battlefield.
- **"Mice"** have shelter and **"rejoice"**; **"crickets jingle there"** implies music, song and happiness. The use of caesura mimics the narrator's pause after each memory, dwelling on what he used to have and how animals have now surpassed him. Repetition of **"doors"** and **"closed"** stresses the safety of the environment at home, but also the abandonment of those on the battlefield; the use of **"the door"**, not 'a' door, depicts a rejection of the soldiers by all those safely at home.
- Stanza 7 is full of vibrant images of hope and love; **"kind fires"** is homely and warming, the sibilant **"suns smile"** is joyful, and the personification of the sun as smiling on **"child, or field, or fruit"** depicts it as a giver and protector of life.
- **"God's invincible spring"** seems both unbreakable (**"invincible"**) and full of potential (**"spring"**). Yet **"we believe"** creates a tone of doubt, and the fact **"born"** is replaced with **"dying"** suggests religious belief **"seems"** to be fading.
- The final stanza shifts to the future tense. **"Tonight"** foreshadows the pain to come, its inevitability reinforced by **"will"**; **"shrivelling"** and **"puckering"** convey life being drawn from the soldiers, and **"crisp"** is both painful and brittle.

Use in essays on…War; Religion; Nature; Fear; Futility; Identity

Storm on the Island – Seamus Heaney

Interpretation: Nature's power is evident as an island is attacked by the brutal strength of a storm. Conflict between nature and the community mean islanders come together to survive as best they can. The poem could also be a metaphor for the brutal violence of the Troubles in Ireland and the effect on local communities.

Form and Structure:
- Blank verse and the controlled use of iambic pentameter, alongside the direct address to the reader (**"you know what I mean"** and **"You might think"**) gives the first section of the poem a calm, conversational tone, showing human resilience in the face of the storm's power.
- The single stanza structure mimics the houses and island; seemingly simple in design, it is **"squat"** and strong in the face of nature's onslaught.
- There is a volta at line 14; the early stoical nature of the narrator, and the use of words such as **"never troubled"** and **"comfortably"**, are replaced by similes of nature turning from **"like a tame cat"** to something that **"spits"** and **"Turned savage"**. Calmness is replaced by **"fear"**.
- A sense of community in the face of violent threat is created by the narrative voice, shown by the repetition of the first-person pronouns **"we"** and **"us"**.

Analysis:
- The single clause **"We are prepared"** followed by a caesura starts the poem in a strong, defiant mood – the villagers are ready and able to face the storm.
- The narrator emphasises the immense pride that is taken in their house building. **"Squat"** implies they are practical houses rather than aesthetically appealing, with **"build"**, **"sink walls"** and **"roof them"** emphasising the skill in their construction.
- **"Walls"**, **"rock"** and **"good slate"** have connotations of great durability, and their power is accentuated by the strong alliterative **"rock and roof"**.
- A positive tone is maintained in the face of great hardship – **"wizened earth"** suggests nature is docile, and poor farming conditions means they are **"never troubled"**, nor is there anything **"that can be lost"**. The locals are not melancholy

about the situation, but rather are accepting of what they have to live with.

- The positive tone is accentuated by the colloquial language of **"as you see"** – the reader is addressed in a relaxed, calm manner, suggesting we have nothing to fear from the storm.
- **"You know what I mean"** further develops the relationship between poet and reader – we are being spoken to as if we are an equal who understands what human hardship entails.
- The ominous mix of natural beauty and destructive natural power combined in the image of a **"tragic chorus"** highlights the dual nature of the storm.
- The **"chorus"** allows the narrator to **"listen"** and **"forget[ting]"** the storm, whereas **"tragic"** implies **"pummels"** is fated to do incredible damage to the island.
- As the poem progresses, the threat and power of the storm intensifies – the enjambment and caesura stress the violence of **"blast"** which destroys the reassuring associations of **"company"**.
- Storms are natural events, but terms from the semantic field of war emphasise the destructive qualities. **"Blast"** and **"exploding"** depict a battlefield scene, with **"strafes"**, **"salvo"** and **"bombarded"** stressing the incessant nature of a battle.
- This increased tension is repeated later in the poem – **"the sea is company"** is made menacing and threatening by the oxymoronic **"Exploding comfortably"**, which implies the storm thrives in this destructive setting.
- Any lingering suggestion of safety is again removed with a combination of enjambment and caesura to stress the negative **"But no"**.
- The image of people who **"just sit tight"** creates a tone of vulnerability and powerlessness. There is nothing to do apart from wait to let the storm pass, with **"just"** emphasising the inadequacy of the action, **"sit"** being entirely passive, and **"tight"** conveying an image of tension.
- Nature causes islanders to be vulnerable by providing **"no natural shelter"**, and violent language such as **"flung"**, **"spits"** and **"pummels"** highlight a real threat.
- However, the largest fear seems to be of a psychological nature – in reality, the islanders are surrounded by **"space"**, **"empty air"** and **"a huge nothing"**, suggesting it is fear of what *might* happen, rather than what will happen, that is most intimidating.

Use in essays on…Human Control; Nature; Fear; Futility

Bayonet Charge – Ted Hughes

Interpretation: The title 'Bayonet Charge' conveys images of bravery, masculinity and heroism in the face of great danger. However, our soldier is depicted as clumsy and ineffectual, running aimlessly towards a **"green hedge"**, entirely unsure as to what he is doing or why he is doing it.

Form and Structure:

- Free verse and varied line length all contribute to a chaotic tone in the poem. This is not a heroic, regimented charge, but an individual blindly flailing in battle.
- Frequent use of caesura, particularly after words associated with movement (**"running"**, **"almost stopped"** and **"statuary in mid-stride"**), emphasises the faltering, broken progress he is making. His **"charge"** is more of a stumble.
- In contrast, the enjambment, particularly the last four lines of the poem, mimics the blind panic of his movement as he hurtles out of control.
- The first sentence, 12 lines long, spans two stanzas, and is full of caesura and enjambment, emphasising the frantic nature of the **"charge"**. It comes to an end when he finally questions what the significance of his **"charge"** is.
- Each stanza advances the soldier's understanding of conflict. He moves from panic in stanza 1, through confusion in stanza 2, into an awareness of the horrors of war in the final stanza.
- Despite the repetition of active verbs such as **"running"**, **"stumbling"** and **"plunged"**, he makes no progress. In stanza 1 he is heading **"towards a green hedge"**, but by stanza 3 he is still moving toward the same **"green hedge"**.

Analysis:

- The man is not a heroic solider – **"suddenly he awoke"** implies he was in a state of slumber, with **"running"** seeming aimless and futile as opposed to **"charge"**.
- The alliteration of 's' 'r' and 'h' sounds in the first three lines are heavy and cumbersome, imitating the soldier's movements; they are not fluid or controlled. This is accentuated by the deep 'o' sound in **"across"** and **"clods"** – by stanza 3, the heavy movement is still evident in the alliteration of **"plunged past"**.
- **"Raw"** alludes to the soldier's inexperience, but also creates a painful, exposed image – even the clothes, meant to protect, are **"raw-seamed"**, with **"seamed"** emphasising the idea they could rip apart at any moment.
- This use of poor equipment is accentuated by his rifle. **"Bayonet Charge"** implies a controlled, deliberate movement

designed to impale enemies. However, he **"lugged"** the rifle, suggesting it is held behind him, ineffectual and clumsy.

- The simile **"numb as a smashed arm"** suggests the weapon is useless – he couldn't use it even if he knew how.
- Even **"air"** becomes corrupted. Rather than give life, it becomes another victim, with destructive **"bullets smacking the belly out"** of it. The corruption of air is complete in stanza 3; it becomes an enemy, **"blue"** and **"crackling"**.
- The juxtaposition of abstract patriotism and brutal reality is clear. A singular **"patriotic tear"** becomes intense **"molten iron"**; the gentle **"brimmed"** becomes **"sweating"**; the **"eye"** it affected has now consumed **"the centre of his chest"**.
- Confusion permeates war. In stanza 2 he is **"in bewilderment"**, **"running"** has **"almost stopped"**, and later he is **"still running"** but does not know the **"reason"**. In the grand scheme of the world **("nations")**, time **("the hand")** or the universe **("stars")**, we are an insignificant nothing – just a **"second"**, gone in an instant.
- Heartless associations of **"cold"**, accentuated by alliteration of **"cold clockwork"**, stress the ceaseless turning of time, and the lack of feeling fate has for humans. **"He was running/Like a man"** implies he is no longer aware of himself as an individual; he has no control over his actions but instead is just **"listening"**.
- Even when the actions seem controlled **("jumped up")** he is still **"in the dark"**, both literally but also figuratively. He is **"in the dark"** as to what he is doing – he has no comprehension as to the purpose of his actions.
- Conflict destroys our control over nature. An expertly ploughed **"field of clods"** has men **"stumbling"** across it; skilfully produced **"furrows"** are **"shot-slashed"**, the sibilance accentuating the speed with which the furrows are destroyed.
- The vibrant **"green hedge"** is destroyed by the violent, unnatural **"rifle fire"**; the **"yellow hare"**, quick and nimble, has been caught and now **"rolled like a flame"**. The rabbit's torture is accentuated by the fact that, rather than feast upon the **"threshing circle"**, it now simply **"crawls"**.
- A sense of hearing is frequently referenced. In stanza 1 a soldier is **"hearing"** bullets; in stanza 2 he is **"listening between his footfalls"**; in stanza 3 the rabbit is **"mouth wide/Open silent"**. Everyone is urgently listening for answers.
- **"Etcetera"** completes a list of three abstract, meaningless ideas **("King, honour, human dignity")** creating a dismissive tone towards traditional images of warfare.
- **"Dropped like luxuries"** confirms the uselessness of these abstract ideas on the reality of the battlefield.
- The solider has been consumed by war and turned into a weapon – his **"terror['s]"** has made him ready to explode like **"dynamite"**.

Use in essays on…Human Control; War; Fear; Futility; Identity

Remains – Simon Armitage

Interpretation: Traditional images of warfare and conflict permeate the poem; Armitage also focuses on the haunting effects of Post-Traumatic Stress Disorder. The power the soldier held in the conflict situation has been replaced by an inability to erase the horrors of death and human destruction from his mind.

Form and Structure:
- The use of varied line length, lack of rhyme scheme and informal language gives the narrative voice a colloquial tone, as if the poem is an anecdote between friends, humanising the 'hero' of the poem.
- The volta at the start of the fifth stanza shifts the narrative from a collective to a singular focus. The pronouns **"we"**, **"us"** and **"we've"** stress a shared responsibility, with the internal rhyme of **"mind"** and **"kind"** drawing the soldiers together as one.
- After the volta, the repeated use of singular pronouns **"I"** and **"my"** suggests the soldiers may work together, but conflict causes isolation and segregation despite supposed comradeship.
- The poem ends with a couplet that stresses the **"bloody"**, physical (**"knuckle"**, **"life"** and **"hands"**) and ever-present (**"here and now"**) nature of war.

Analysis:
- **"On another occasion"** immediately stresses the effects of conflict are not one-off incidents, but rather a series of continual events and incidents – the reader has entered mid-story, and we are being introduced to the fact this is **"another"** tale.
- **"We get sent out"** dehumanises the narrator – he is seen as a tool of war, no different to a vehicle or weapon, called upon by a faceless authority.
- The hesitant tone of **"probably armed, possibly not"**, enhanced by the alliterative "p", implies doubt and uncertainty in the narrator's mind, an idea that haunts the narrator repeatedly. Whilst **"probably"** provides some level of certainty, the phrase ends on the far more doubtful **"possibly"**.
- War is not heroic – the informality of **"looters"** suggests a simple threat level, enhanced by the juvenile image of **"legs it"** and **"carted off"**.

- The alliterative **"my mates"** is an image of togetherness, but the list of **"myself and somebody else and somebody else"** implies a collective of individuals, not a cohesive group.
- **"All of the same mind"**, **"all three of us"** and **"three of a kind"** implies a common purpose, yet **"the same mind"** suggests brainwashing, a robotic response to an order to kill.
- Mise-en-page stresses **"I see"**, with the narrator's precise recall of events then reinforced by depictions of clarity and lucidity in **"every round"** and **"broad daylight"**.
- The narrator is fully aware of his actions and the surroundings, but this lucidity will later haunt him when **"I close my eyes"**.
- The violent "r" and "t" sound in **"rips"** and **"torn apart"** intensifies the fragility of **"life"** – it was a living person, not just an unidentifiable body or enemy, who died.
- The confused **"sort of inside out"** stresses the incomprehensibility of war, with its dehumanising nature increased by the dismissive tone of **"tosses his guts"**.
- **"Pain"** and **"agony"** are personified - these elements of conflict are no longer abstract nouns, but rather living depictions of suffering with their own **"guts"**.
- Conflict never leaves the narrator – **"shadow"** implies both a haunting and a sense it is ever-present, but **"blood-shadow"** gives the shadow substance, depth and colour.
- **"Home"**, **"sleep"** and **"dream"** should provide peace and sanctuary for the narrator but are destroyed by the violent connotations of **"burst"** and the plosive "b" in **"bursts...bank"**. **"Again"** suggests the never-ending nature of the conflict.
- The alliterative **"drink"** and **"drugs"** stresses the narrator's desperation; he has a need to **"flush him out"**, with **"flush"** implying a desperation to be cleansed.
- The alliterative **"he's here in my head"** accentuates the inescapable nature of conflict; the **"enemy"** is not other soldiers, but war itself.
- Sibilance in **"sun-stunned, sand-smothered"**, alongside violent images of **"stunned"** and **"smothered"**, implies nature has become hostile and oppressive.

Use in essays on…Global Conflict; Appearance vs Reality; Time; War; Weakness

Poppies – Jane Weir

Interpretation: It is unclear as to whether Weir's absent child has left for war, passed away in conflict, or has simply left home, but the internal struggle and sense of loss she feels is equally intense in all three situations.

Form and Structure:

- The free verse and direct address to **"you"** creates a personal, intimate monologue. The sense of isolation is enhanced as **"you"** never responds.
- The chronological narrative follows the change in the woman's behaviour. Once the child leaves, active behaviours of the first three stanzas are replaced in the final stanza by the passive **"leaned"**, **"listened"** and **"hoping"**. She is no longer in control and yearns for a return of the youthful **"playground voice"** that worries of nothing but childhood games.
- The long, multi-clause sentences and flow from stanza 2 to 3, combined with adventurous associations of the simile **"like a treasure chest"** and endless prospects of **"world overflowing"**, depict the magnitude of the moment.
- In contrast, the enjambment and sibilance of **"split second"** highlights the speed with which the child moves away from the mother.

Analysis:

- The national remembrance of **"Armistice Sunday"** is juxtaposed with the personal suffering of **"individual war graves"**. Although honouring heroism and bravery, the caesura places focus on **"war graves"** and the links with death.
- Whether referencing a boy going off to war or simply a child growing up and leaving home, the stress on **"you left"** creates a tone of loss.
- **"Crimped"** suggests care and skill in turning a delicate **"petal"** into a poppy, implying the respect that goes into making them. However, **"petal"** could refer to the vulnerable young men who were forcefully recruited (**"crimped"**) into war.
- Numerous images of maternal tenderness also contain language that alludes to danger or harm. The vibrant **"paper red"** is juxtaposed with the violent **"spasms"**, giving the **"red"** connotations of blood rather than positivity.
- The **"blazer"** is a symbol of respect and dignity, but the **"yellow bias binding"** has restrictive associations due to the military term **"blockade"**, as if the blazer is oppressing the child – the mother feels the need to **"disrupting"** it.
- The domestic, playful **"white cat hairs"** suggest tenderness between cat and owner. They are **"rounded up"** as if they were criminals, done with **"bandaged"** **"Sellotape"**, implying these hairs, a sign of love and family life, are a wound.

- The mother's actions, whilst protective, are simple gestures of love rather than actively keeping the child safe. **"I pinned one"** and **"smoothed down your shirt's/upturned collar"** are intimate but relatively meaningless.
- The sibilant **"steeled the softening"** reinforces the conflicted nature of the relationship. Whilst she wants to be soft and gentle, instead she **"steeled"** her face, trying to maintain a cold, hard exterior.
- Even the sensual, tactile image of **"graze my nose/across the tip of your nose"**, a loving, tender act, is tainted by the painful associations of **"graze"**. Whilst the idea of **"being Eskimos"** is fun and playful, there is a tone of sadness. They **"play at"**, highlighting childhood is just a game, reinforced by **"when/you were little"**, stressing the temporary, fleeting nature of parent/child relationships.
- **"Run my fingers"** is a tender act that is out of place in this situation; **"gelled"** suggests the child is maturing, with **"blackthorns"** giving him a hardened edge.
- The tri-colon of verbs **"flattened, rolled, turned"** all suggest the changing nature of the relationship – the enjambment between stanzas 2 and 3 stresses the unstoppable nature of this change until it is **"melting"** away, never to return.
- It is not only in warfare that we see bravery – **"I was brave"** is a defiant statement asserting the strength needed to let a child go.
- There is a juxtaposition between the new world of the **"intoxicated"** young man, suggesting overwhelmed, enthralled, perhaps drunken or out of control, and the controlled domestic setting of a mother **"making tucks, darts, pleats"**.
- The creativity and joy of **"song bird"**, as well as the pure beauty of **"dove"**, symbolises the importance of **"a single"** solitary bird finding its own way in life. **"Released"** and **"cage"** allude to freedom, with the fricative "f" in **"flew from"** reinforcing the flight and journey of the boy.
- **"Hat"**, **"winter coat"** or **"scarf, gloves"** are **"reinforcements"**, but are all a mother can provide; they are useless as military support. The setting of the **"war memorial"** reminds the reader of the dangers that are to be faced in life, particularly when alone and exposed at **"the top of the hill"**.
- The parent/child relationship, symbolised by the **"wishbone"**, is joined together, full of hope, but for the wish to come true, the **"wishbone"** must be pulled apart.
- When given the freedom the **"dove pulled freely"**, suggesting without restriction, and in the vast **"sky"** it takes the opportunity to create something beautiful (**"ornamental stitch"**).

Use in essays on… Human Control; Family Conflict; Time; Fear

War Photographer – Carol Ann Duffy

Interpretation: War is unflinching – the photographer must record the brutal reality of war with professionalism and compassion, cataloguing the very worst of human behaviour whilst also providing support in people's most vulnerable moments. In **"Rural England"** we have the power to sanitise this experience – we are moved to gentle tears, but do not expand our understanding.

Form and Structure:

- Regular stanza length and a consistent rhyme scheme convey calmness and composure, mimicking the photographer's approach to his work. The action may be graphic, but he remains composed throughout.
- The use of caesura **("He has a job to do.")** and short sentences **("Belfast. Beirut. Phnom Penh.")** create a tone of religious incantation, as if the photographer's role has a spiritual significance, reinforced by the biblical allusion **"All flesh is grass"**.
- The narrative voice turns at the beginning of the third stanza; the professional tone of a man with **"a job to do"** changes as **"something is happening"** and he becomes angry and resentful of those who **"do not care"**.

Analysis:

- A war photographer has an almost spiritual power, implied by the religious associations of **"church"**, **"priest"** and **"Mass"**.
- However, religious images are not all positive – **"ordered rows"** depicts the care of the photographer trying to bring order to the chaos of war, but could also allude to **"ordered rows"** of graves, as if he is trying to bring the victims some dignity in death.
- War inevitably brings death, and there is a haunting tone to the poem; **"darkroom"** and the **"red"** light are threatening, and the horror in the **"spools of suffering"** is accentuated by the sinister sibilance.
- The plural **"spools"** highlights the scale of conflict; whilst he is **"finally alone"**, there is no sanctuary from war.
- Contrasting the isolation of the **"darkroom"**, the reader sees that war plagues the entire planet, with single word sentences, syllable structure and the plosive "b" and "p" in **"Belfast. Beirut. Phnom Penh."** creating an intensely violent tone.

- The photographer is clinical in his role, shown through the monosyllabic, single clause, **"He has a job to do"**, yet he seems nervous back home. The sibilant, **"solutions slop"** mimic spillage, and **"slop"** and **"tremble"** emphasise a lack of control.
- **"Rural England"** is unaware of the realities of the world. The tone of **"fields"**, **"ordinary pain"** and **"simple weather"** is condescending, especially in contrast with the brutal imagery of **"explode"**, **"running children"** and **"nightmare heat"**.
- The loss of individuality and the ambiguity of war are stressed by **"stranger's features"**, **"faintly"**, and by **"half-formed ghost"**; **"ghost"** also references the afterlife alluded to in the first stanza, reminding the reader that for all of the photographer's work, his subjects are still dead.
- However, despite not knowing who these people are, the photographer's memories are also vivid and sensual. **"Features"** appear **"before his eyes"** (visual memory), and he **"remembers the cries"** (aural memory).
- The importance of war photography is stressed through the imperative tone of **"do what someone must"**.
- He gives identity to the anonymous (**"this man's wife"**), communicates the incomprehensible (**"without words"**) and restores dignity to those who suffer (**"sought approval"**).
- Whilst **"blood"** highlights the explicit brutality of war, and **"stained"** its lasting impact, **"foreign dust"** accentuates the distance between the reader and conflict, with **"aeroplane"** in the final stanza reinforcing the separation between the reader and the victims of war.
- Emotive **"agonies"** are explicitly depicted in **"black and white"**, yet **"Rural England"** needs war to be sanitised. **"Hundred"** is juxtaposed with **"five or six"**, and the sibilant **"Sunday's supplement"** belittles the **"cries"** that were heard.
- The readers seem uncaring. Their **"eyeballs"** respond, not their heart, and **"prick/with tears"** is an unsympathetic response to the previous **"cries"**.
- Indeed, the image of **"bath"** and **"pre-lunch beers"** quickly erase the sorrow and seem inappropriately pleasant activities after viewing such horrors.
- Our response as people living in **"Rural England"** is inadequate. It is simply a **"living"** for the photographer, and we **"do not care"**.

Use in essays on…Global Conflict; War; Appearance vs Reality; Identity

Tissue – Imtiaz Dharker

Interpretation: Tissue explores the fragile yet powerful nature of paper as a record of humanity, as well as alluding to human tissue and its temporary nature; tissue becomes a metaphor for what it is to be human. Are we restricted by paper controls (money, maps and rules) or does paper allow creative freedom to **"shine through"**?

Form and Structure:
- The reader is presented with the idea that paper has the power to cast light and illuminate, an idea that is frequently revisited. The alliterative **"lets the light"** combined with enjambment mimics the persistent flow of light that **"shine[s] through"**.
- In the first section of the poem, the verbs **"smoothed"**, **"stroked"** and **"turned"** have associations with care, reinforced by the calm tone and gentle rhythm created by the sibilance and asyndetic list, implying paper that records humanity is more than an inanimate object – it inspires tenderness in the reader.
- However, after the second sentence, **"buildings"** is the first reference to the rigid man-made objects that restrict human nature, which is later reinforced by the inflexible associations of **"brick/or block"** and accentuated by the harsh, plosive "b".
- The final single line stanza confirms the power of **"tissue"**. Be it paper tissue or human tissue, it defines the essence of who we are as it **"turned into your skin"**.

Analysis:
- The power of paper is not certain – the verb **"could"** implies change is not guaranteed, and the abstract **"things"** suggests it is unclear what it will **"alter"**.
- **"Thinned"** has fragile associations yet paper is integral to humanity. **"Thinned by age or touching"** implies it is revered, holding power over religious (**"Koran"**), historical (**"names and histories"**) and personal (**"born to whom"**) beliefs.
- **"Height and weight, who/died where and how"** gives a personal, detailed history of humanity; **"sepia date"** confirms paper's resilience to record human life long after **"living tissue"** has gone. Paper may fade but is stronger than human tissue.

- **"Smoothed and stroked"** reinforces the respect shown to paper and suggests our relationship with paper mimics the bond between parent and child.
- **"Buildings"** conflict with paper's flexibility; internal rhyme connects **"drift"** and **"shift"**, with **"sigh"** and **"wind"** completing the image of movement and fluidity.
- The tone of the short single clause sentence **"Maps too"** is dismissive of the use of paper to create **"roads"** and **"railtracks"**. These unnatural constructs are used by humans to exert control, much like **"borderlines"** that are barriers that frequently cause conflict.
- Nature's beautiful **"rivers"** and **"mountainfolds"** are reduced to **"marks"** when put on maps for reasons of control, but still **"the sun shines through"**.
- A semantic field of money (**"shops"**, **"how much was sold"**, **"paid by credit card"**) implies paper is used by institutions to control us. A receipt might be seemingly innocent **"fine slips"**, but they are symbolic of economic ownership.
- **"Fine slips"** can also tell imaginative tales about the beauty of human experience; the simile **"fly our lives like paper kites"** conveys freedom and childish joy.
- **"Layer over layer"** implies a multi-faceted approach to building within society, with the delicate **"place"** suggesting care and attention to detail.
- The tri-colon **"script over numbers over line"** depicts the blending of language (**"script"**), maths (**"numbers"**) and art (**"line"**) that paper provides; as a building material, it provides light to many structures (**"luminous"** and **"daylight break"**).
- This contrasts the harsh, rigid **"capitals and monoliths"**. These are simply non-descript **"shapes"** we foolishly build not for beauty, but for our shallow **"pride"**.
- Enjambment between stanzas 8 and 9 implies the creation of perfection (**"grand design"**) has already been achieved; it is built with **"living tissue"**.
- The impermanence and temporary nature of human life (it was **"never meant to last"**) is what bestows value upon it. The tri-colon **"smoothed and stroked and turned"** from stanza 3 has become **"thinned"**, suggesting that it is gradually fading away.

Use in essays on…Religion; Human Control; Identity; Time; Global Conflict

The Emigrée – Carol Rumens

Interpretation: Rumens' **"city"** might be a literal place, or a metaphor for a specific person, time or event. Whatever interpretation, Rumens holds an unwaveringly positive, sun-filled view of the **"city"**, and she is unmoved by any suggestion, however threatening, that her positive views are no longer correct or welcome.

Form and Structure:
- The use of free verse and the conversational, story-like tone of **"there once was"** depicts the narrator as relaxed and comfortable in nature, resisting the images of oppression throughout the poem.
- The image of sunlight permeates the poem and evolves from stanza to stanza. As the poem develops, the image of memory being bright, powerful **"sunlight"** intensifies. In stanza 1 it is an **"impression"** – an idea or thought. In stanza 2 it **"tastes of sunlight"** – it has become sensual and physical.
- By stanza 3 her **"shadow falls as evidence of sunlight"**, with **"evidence"** suggesting she is living, breathing proof of her city's brightness.
- The repetition of the conjunction **"but"** throughout the poem and in every stanza enhances the conflict throughout the poem – the narrator is meant to hold one view, **"but"** refuses to be told what to think.

Analysis:
- The sentence structure of the first line, **"there once was a country"**, stresses the past tense – the **"country"** she mentions is no longer there.
- **"Left"** and **"child"** suggest the narrator's memories of her country could have since faded, or be incomplete, yet her **"memory"** is **"sunlight-clear"**, with **"clear"** emphasising the unclouded nature of her memories.
- Vibrant, illuminating associations of **"sunlight"** stress the positive tone of these memories.
- The narrator has a tone of scepticism towards any negative views of her city. She sees it as **"the mildest city"**, with associations of temperance and pleasantness; others see it with the dark, cold connotations of **"November"**.
- The narrator maintains a defiant tone, and **"It seems"** and **"I am told"** imply the narrator does not believe these alternate views of her city.

- The use of the metaphor **"bright, filled paperweight"** suggests the narrator's memories are clear (**"bright"**), plentiful (**"filled"**) and strong in nature (**"paperweight"**), all safely enclosed within the paperweight and unmoved by any external influence.
- The reality is that the city she loves is clearly in a troubled state. It is full of conflict (**"at war"**), disease (**"sick"**) and oppression (**"tyrants"**), yet her **"original view"** is **"branded"** on her, depicting an image permanently imprinted on her mind.
- The narrator's city is pure (**"white streets"**), elegant (**"graceful slopes"**), and resilient to conflict (**"time rolls its tanks"** and **"frontiers rise between us"**).
- The perspective the narrator views her city from may well be perceived as **"hollow"** and **"a lie"** to the authorities (**"they"**) – the city is now a **"state"**, with associations of strict governmental power enforced by the oppressive, threatening tone of **"banned"**.
- However, her **"child's vocabulary"** brings an innocent view of the city, and the state has no control over her memories. She is sensually overwhelmed by their intensity as she has **"every coloured molecule"** and **"can't get it off my tongue"**, with **"coloured"** stressing the clarity of her memories, and **"tongue"** implying that the memories cause a physical reaction in her.
- The mental freedoms the narrator enjoys in the first two stanzas are then replaced by a variety of physical restrictions at the beginning of the third stanza. The repetition of **"no"** in **"no passport, there's no way back"** stresses her inability to return.
- Much like a pet, child or partner, her city provides intimate support (**"comes to me"**), tenderness (**"lies down in front of me"**) and joy (**"takes me dancing"**), whilst she treats it with love and affection (**"comb its hair and love its shining eyes"**).
- Repetition of **"accuse"** highlights the threatening reality of the city, reinforced by images of confinement (**"walls"** and **"circle"**) and threats (**"mutter death"**).
- The relationship is mutually beneficial – whilst the city provides the narrator with **"sunlight"**, she protects its beauty as it **"hides behind me"** for safety.

Use in essays on…Global Conflict; Oppression; Identity; Individuals vs Society

Checking Out Me History – John Agard

Interpretation: Agard explores how history is a one-sided interpretation of the past, designed to reinforce a world view **"they"** want you to hear; it also attempts to erase any history that may be relevant and meaningful to the less powerful in society.

Form and Structure:

- Repetition of **"Dem tell me"** throughout the poem mimics the incessant wave of **"History"** imposed upon the narrator. The faceless **"dem"** implies the narrator has no connection to those teaching him, nor the history taught; the plural **"dem"** is juxtaposed with the singular pronoun **"me"**, stressing his isolation.

- By the final stanza, the passive **"me"** is repeated but ultimately rejected – **"me"** becomes the far more powerful **"I"**, strengthening Agard's sense of identity.

- The simplistic rhyme scheme and four-line structure of stanzas depicting British **"history"** stresses the unimaginative and uninspiring nature of this education. In contrast, the free verse, varied stanza length and short, emphatic sentence lengths of stanzas exploring Agard's history have a vibrant, engaging tone.

- The constant juxtaposition of scientific and historical figures in the same sentence as childish nursery rhymes or fictional tales stresses Agard's message – that 'British' history has as much relevance to him as fictional material.

Analysis:

- **"Bandage"** has associations with healing and protection; here it is an image of restriction. The plosive 'b' in **"bandage"** and **"blind"** has an aggressive tone, implying **"dem"** are controlling Agard's body (**"bandage"**) and what information he has access to (**"blind"**) – they are physically hiding his history from view.

- **"1066"**, full of historical significance, is reduced by the dismissive tone of **"all dat"**. The rhyming couplet links **"1066 and all dat"** with **"Dick Whittington and he cat"**, implying 1066 is no more significant than pantomime folklore.

- **"Florence Nightingale"** is only defined by **"she lamp"** and mentioned alongside **"Robin Hood"** and his **"camp"**, reducing historical figures to nothing more than mythical tales in Agard's eyes.

- British education focuses on the fictional **"ole King Cole"** and his irrelevant **"merry ole soul"** but the incredible achievements of **"Mary Seacole"** are omitted.

- **"Lord Nelson and Waterloo"** are of great significance but the use of **"de great"** in **"Shaka de great Zulu"** emphasises the personal connection Agard feels towards these unexplored historical figures.

- Education is about understanding and exploration – **"Columbus and 1492"** are covered, but the lack of focus on **"de Caribs and de Arawaks"** is accentuated by the questioning of **"but what happen"**.
- **"Discover"** conveys scientific advances; the unnamed **"man"** lessens its importance, reinforced by the rhyme scheme combining this achievement with **"de cow who jump over de moon"** and **"de dish ran away with de spoon"**.
- The lack of significance is accentuated by the nameless **"man who discover de balloon"** in comparison with the clear identity of **"Nanny de maroon"**.
- The italicised stanzas convey the message that unlike British history, Agard's history is not one-dimensional. Rather than defining Toussant as **"a slave"**, he is described as having **"vision"**, focusing on his intellectual, strategic prowess.
- He is **"de thorn"** to **"de French"** but also **"de beacon/of de Haitian Revolution"**, explicitly exploring the varied nature of historical interpretation.
- History should use one's own language to give it legitimacy. **"Lick back"** is more appropriate for Agard than 'defeated'; **"Nanny"** is a **"see-far woman"** rather than 'insightful'. Language and context combine to make history relatable.
- British history is about names **("Lord Nelson")**, dates **("1066"/"1492")** and facts, but Agard's history is sensual, emotive and creative. The nouns **"mountain"**, **"stream"** and **"river"** connect people with their environment, whilst the abstract **"dream"**, **"hopeful"** and **"freedom"** accentuates the motivations behind their historical actions.
- People aren't defined by events but by intrinsic characteristics; **"Nanny"** is shown with the image of a **"fire-woman"**, **"fire"** implying her burning passion in her **"struggle"**. Mary Seacole displays the traditional heroic qualities of a soldier **"when de British said no"** yet **"she still brave the Russian snow"**.
- A multi-faceted history is completed by the metaphorical description of Seacole - **"star"** and **"sunrise"** connect her with the universe, whilst **"healing"** stresses her care and medical skill, combined with the vibrancy and vitality of **"yellow"**.
- In the final stanza, Agard has a passive role in **"Dem tell me"**, with its oppressive connotations reinforced by **"wha dem want"**. However, he ends by taking ownership of his past, with **"checking out"** implying a more relaxed, engaged exploration than **"tell"**.
- **"Checking"** also implies he will question and validate history, rather than blindly accept. **"Carving"** has an even more active implication – Agard is physically altering and shaping **"me identity"** into something permanent.

Use in essays on…Individuals vs Society; Oppression; Identity; Misuse of Power

Kamikaze – Beatrice Garland

Interpretation: War creates internal as well as external conflict. A kamikaze pilot's duty to his country conflicts with a love of life and his family; in choosing life, he is brutally rejected by all around him when he returns. In a battle between an individual and society, society holds all the power.

Form and Structure:
- The weight of emotion in a kamikaze situation is illustrated by the poem's structure. The first five stanzas are a single sentence, with enjambment rapidly connecting one thought to another, conveying a stream of hurried thoughts.
- Interruption from punctuation or pauses are rare in the poem; even the interruption **"yes, grandfather's boat"** is quickly dismissed, mimicking the incessant thought process both pilot and narrator go through.
- The third-person narrator seems overwhelmed by a barrage of conflicting emotions. The first-person narration of stanzas 6 and 7 is slower in rhythm, with more frequent pauses, creating a more thoughtful, calming tone.

Analysis:
- Despite the isolation of the Kamikaze pilot on his return, the poem begins with the strong familial connection of **"her father"**.
- **"Embarked at sunrise"** has the tone of a heroic, mythical journey, with **"sunrise"** alluding to the great traditions and history of Japan.
- The pilot is immersed in this heritage. **"Samurai sword"** symbolises a connection to Japanese warriors of the past; he also conforms to militaristic (**"shaven head"**), religious (**"powerful incantations"**) and political (**"journey into history"**) expectations of his country.
- **"Flask of water"**, **"enough fuel"** and **"one-way"** highlight that this man is not prepared for an epic battle but is instead on a **"one-way"** suicide mission.
- Kamikaze pilots destroy ships, but here boats are positive symbols. **"Fishing boats"** imply sustenance; **"father's boat"** alongside **"grandfather's boat"** depict boats bringing people together, not tearing them apart.
- Furthermore, the simile **"strung out like bunting"** alongside the repetition of **"safe"** creates a celebratory image of family that convinces the pilot to turn back.

- The isolation of kamikaze missions is contrasted with welcoming images of family companionship. **"His brothers waiting on the shore"** are an image of gentleness and togetherness, and they **"built cairns"**; **"built"** has association with creation, not destruction.
- The imagery of **"withstood longest/the turbulent inrush of breakers"** stresses a resistance towards aggression and conflict, rather than being the cause of it.
- Rather than the destructive **"one-way"** movement, fish move in beautiful, fluid ways. **"Arcing in swathes"** combines both freedom and unity, and the sibilant **"swivelled towards the sun"** links the fluid, rhythmical movement of the fish with life-giving illumination.
- These natural movements act as a **"huge flag"** of warning, as if the natural world wishes to halt the kamikaze mission – the world has so much positivity in it (**"strung out like bunting"**) that it seems inconceivable that someone would wish to destroy it.
- The beautiful, sensual and vibrant nature of the **"green-blue translucent sea"**, **"flashing silver"** and **"loose silver"**, alongside the multitude of fish in stanza 5, depicts a natural world that is teeming with a variety of sea life that exists in harmony with one another.
- The tri-colon **"dark prince, muscular, dangerous"** stresses the deadly nature of the **"tuna, the dark prince"**, but it still co-exists with others rather than destroys.
- The innocent **"chattered and laughed"** of the children contrasts the powerful adult propaganda of **"powerful incantations"**.
- **"Gradually"**, **"learned"** and **"as though"** imply resistance to the idea **"he had never returned"**. They refuse to forget this is **"the father we loved"**.
- The pilot is completely rejected. **"Never"** and **"again"** stress the permanence of his rejection; verbal (**"spoke"**) and emotional (**"meet his eyes"**) bonds are broken.
- Although **"silent"**, the narrator is defiant. **"She thought"** implies he never left her mind, and **"recounting it later to her children"** keeps his memory alive.
- In conflict situations, death takes many forms, but it is inevitable – **"the better way to die"** compares a bodily death with a mental death.

Use in essays on…Family Conflict; Time; Identity; War; Individuals vs Society

Major Themes

Human Control	Global Conflict	Family Conflict
Individuals vs Society	Misuse of Power	Appearance vs Reality
Weakness	War	Religion
Nature	Fear	Oppression
Futility	Time	Identity

How to revise effectively.

One mistake people often make is to try to revise EVERYTHING! This is clearly not possible.

Instead, once you understand the poems, a great idea is to group the poems, then pick three or four major themes, and then revise these in great detail. If, for example, you revised War, Nature or Religion, you will also have covered a huge amount of material to use in questions about Futility or Global Conflict.

Or, if you revised Family or Identity, you would certainly have plenty of material if a question on the misuse of power, Oppression or Human Control was set.

Use the following framework as a basis for setting *any* of your own revision questions – simply swap the theme to create a new essay title!

Compare how poets present ideas about (a theme) in (a poem) and in one other poem from Power and Conflict.

A sample essay style paragraph (top level), using ideas directly from The Quotation Bank (page 17 and 23).

Compare how poets present fear in Remains and in one other poem from Power and Conflict.

Conflict never leaves the narrator, and its presence causes fear to grow – **"shadow"** implies he is haunted, but **"blood-shadow"** gives the shadow depth, substance and colour, an even more fearful image. **"Home"**, **"sleep"** and **"dream"** should provide peace and safety but are destroyed by the violent connotations of **"burst"** and the plosive "b" in **"bursts...bank"**; **"again"** further suggests conflict's never-ending fear has infiltrated his mind. The idea of being haunted by fear is also evident in Owen's *Exposure*, and much like Armitage, the sanctuary of home does nothing to alleviate that fear. Indeed, for Owen, memories of home increase the suffering. **"Ghosts"** implies soldiers are already resigned to death; rather than being released freely into the afterlife, **"slowly"** alongside **"drag"** implies even in death they are burdened and weary, reinforced by the elongated 'o' sound in **"slowly"**, **"ghosts"** and **"home"**. Unlike Owen, for whom there is no escape from fear, Armitage turns to **"drink"** and **"drugs"** to try to overcome it. The alliterative **"drink"** and **"drugs"** stresses his desperation; he has a need to **"flush him out"**, with **"flush"** implying the need to be cleansed. Furthermore, the alliterative **"he's here in my head"** depicts the inescapable nature of conflict; the **"enemy"** is not other soldiers, but war itself, and it is this mental anguish that he fears, rather than any physical threat.

Potential Essay Style Questions

Compare how poets present the effects of war in *Bayonet Charge* and in one other poem from Power and Conflict.

Bayonet Charge: War is frequently depicted as heroic, brave and patriotic, with power being bestowed upon the victors. However, Hughes depicts the true effects of war – it brings death and disorder, and replaces patriotism with chaos and fear.

Poems for potential comparison:

The Charge of the Light Brigade: War exposes the fact that those in power don't care for their men; they are simply tools of war. It also proves that power does not mean responsibility; those who wield it are unworthy of it, using it without care or thought.

War Photographer: The effects of war are polarising; on one hand, it forges intimate human connections that transcend race, religion or language. On the other, geographical distance means that whilst for some war is real, others "do not care".

Remains: War brings physical pain and suffering, yet it can cause a far greater conflict in terms of mental anguish and destruction. During combat, power seems to lie with the soldiers, but the long-term effects of war makes victims of all involved.

Compare how poets present the misuse of power in *London* and in one other poem from Power and Conflict.

London: London is an immensely powerful city, but the reality of the "chartered Thames" is that religious, governmental and military institutions are abusing the city for their own selfish gains, causing immense suffering to "every man" within it.

Poems for potential comparison:

My Last Duchess: Marriage as an arrangement between powerful families was common, but the Duke misuses the power of his "nine-hundred-years-old name" to control his wife's life, behaviour, friendships and eventually, her death.

The Emigrée: The bond between a person and their country should be a personal one, unburdened by outside forces, yet the narrator finds that powerful elements are infringing upon her own relationship, misusing their power to influence and control.

Checking Out Me History: History should be an unbiased view of the past, with all elements of humanity explored. However, Agard finds that, as a young boy in a new country, education and history are controlled by those with an agenda to maintain, denying him access to his true heritage whilst promoting their own views.

Compare how poets present the conflict between man and nature in *Exposure* and in one other poem from Power and Conflict.

Exposure: Owen depicts the reality of war and the intense suffering and death it creates, yet he also explores the terrible role nature plays in human anguish – rather than bring safety and protection to those in need, the horrors of "wind", "snow" and "frost" bring pain far greater than any man-made weapon.

Poems for potential comparison:

Extract from, The Prelude: Relationships with nature are frequently formative for humans. Whilst these experiences are often positive and life-affirming, they can also highlight the insignificance of humanity and teach us many lessons; here, nature confirms to us that in any relationship with nature, it is nature that holds the upper hand, and it will use its power to make sure that power dynamic is maintained.

Storm on the Island: The relationship between mankind and nature is a complex one – whilst mankind and nature can co-exist to create a beautiful environment for communities to live and flourish in, mankind must understand the need to respect nature; we have no control over its raw and indiscriminate power.

Compare how poets present the effects of time on power in *Ozymandias* and in one other poem from Power and Conflict.

Ozymandias: Ozymandias views himself as "king of kings", yet time rapidly erodes his power until he is nothing more than a "colossal wreck" – it is art and the natural world that can stand the test of time, not any form of human power.

Poems for potential comparison:

Poppies: Parents use whatever is in their power to protect their children, yet it is inevitable that, step by step, time will remove a child from their control until the child is "gone" and parents are left "hoping", the most futile of actions.

Tissue: Time erodes memories, history and human tissue; whatever power did exist fades. However, paper has the power to defeat time; by recording memories, history and human greatness, it can shed "light" on the world, past, present and future.

Kamikaze: Kamikaze pilots were seen as patriotic, and their duty was, in one single moment, to serve their country. Yet the time it took to fly a mission causes the power of patriotism to be replaced by the fear of death and the love of one's family, a decision that then haunts the pilot forever.

Suggested Revision Activities

Major themes and comparisons – Pick one of the major themes (see page 36 for a list) and group 3 or 4 poems together as a cluster that might be useful in answering on that theme. Next, for each poem, select 10 to 12 quotations that focus on that theme. At least 3 quotations should refer to form and structure.

Group the quotations in a 'theme within a theme'. For example, if you selected 10-12 quotations on nature in Exposure, you could group them as follows:

- Quotations that depict nature as an active enemy to the soldiers

- Quotations that highlight nature's complete disregard for humanity

- Quotations about nature that depict the peace and comfort in life away from war.

Finally, plan which poems could work together to answer an exam question on your chosen theme.

The Development Game – Select a poem and create an essay question for it. Next, pick a quotation from the poem and use it to create a focused topic sentence to start the essay.

Next, find another appropriate quotation to develop your idea even further.

Repeat this until you feel you have a detailed paragraph that answers the question!

Once you have a detailed paragraph, do the same for a different poem, so you have material to use for comparison.

Essay writing – They aren't always fun, but writing essays is great revision. Choose a practice question and then try taking a variety of quotations and writing out a perfect paragraph, making sure you add connectives, technical vocabulary and sophisticated language. Also, make sure the connections you make between the poems are meaningful – just because two poems have a basic connection between them (for instance, there are children in London and in Poppies) does not mean there is a significant point to be made.

Glossary

Alliteration – Repetition of the same consonant or sound at the beginning of a number of words in a sentence to create emphasis: "Do and die" utilises the alliterative 'd' sound to create a heroic tone.

Caesura – A pause or stop within a line of poetry: the single clause "We are prepared" followed by a caesura starts the poem in a strong, defiant mood.

Enjambment – When one line continues on to the next line or stanza without pause: enjambment links "stone" and "stand", creating associations of immobility and passivity.

Imagery – Figurative language that appeals to the senses of the reader: the brutal imagery of "nightmare heat" conveys the physical pain of war.

Irony – A statement that suggests one thing but often has a contrary meaning: the image of a "pedestal" is ironic – designed to elevate Ozymandias above his people, it now contains nothing but empty "words" and stresses how far he has fallen.

Juxtaposition – Two ideas, images or words placed next to each other to create a contrasting effect: juxtaposition between the freedom of "flow" and the restrictive "chartered" emphasises the conflict surrounding London and the Thames.

Language – The vocabulary chosen to create effect.

Metaphor – A word or phrase used to describe something else so that the first idea takes on the associations of the second: the metaphor "bright, filled paperweight" suggests the narrator's memories are clear ("bright"), plentiful ("filled") and strong in nature ("paperweight").

Narrative Voice – The perspective (or 'voice') from which the poem is told: a sense of community in the face of violent threat is created by the narrative voice, shown by the repetition of the first-person pronouns "we" and "us".

Oxymoron – A figure of speech where apparently contradictory terms appear together: the oxymoronic "black with snow" is a vivid image of natural corruption.

Personification – A non-human object or concept takes on human qualities to make its presence more vivid to the reader: "suns smile" is joyful, and the personification of the sun as smiling on "child, or field, or fruit" depicts it as a giver and protector of life.

Repetition – When a word, phrase or idea is repeated to reinforce it: the repetition of "no" emphatically rejects the past relationship.

Rhyme Scheme – The pattern of rhymes or sounds at the end of each line: the ABAB rhyme scheme is relentless, creating a sense of the incessant suffering within the city, and a tone of weariness and depression is accentuated by the rhyme of the deep, heavy vowel sounds.

Semantic Field – A group of words used together from the same topic area: terms from the semantic field of war emphasise the destructive qualities. "Blast" and "exploding" depict a battlefield scene, with "strafes", "salvo" and "bombarded" stressing the incessant nature of a warzone.

Sentence Structure – The way the writer has ordered the words in a sentence to create a certain effect: the sentence structure of the first line, "there once was a country", stresses the past tense – the "country" she mentions is no longer there.

Sibilance – A variation on alliteration, usually of the 's' sound, that creates a hissing sound: sibilance in "sun-stunned,/sand-smothered" implies nature has become hostile and oppressive.

Simile – A comparison of one thing with something of a different kind, used to make a description more vivid: the simile "numb as a smashed arm" suggests the weapon is useless – he couldn't use it even if he knew how.

Symbolism – The use of a symbol to represent an idea: a "church" should symbolise spiritual salvation, yet "black'ning" conveys a corruption within the powerful church establishment.

Tone – The mood or atmosphere created by the poet: the images of "frown", "wrinkled lip" and "sneer" all convey a tone of contempt.

Tri-colon – A list of three words or phrases for effect: the tri-colon "whisper, curious, nervous" conveys fear and tension that infiltrates even the bravest man.

Acknowledgments:

Seamus Heaney *Storm On The Island* from *Opened Ground* by permission of Faber and Faber Ltd.
Ted Hughes *Bayonet Charge* from *Collected Poems* by permission of Faber and Faber Ltd.
Simon Armitage *Remains* © Simon Armitage. Reproduced by permission of the author.
Jane Weir *Poppies* from *The Way I Dressed During the Revolution* by permission of Templar Poetry
War Photographer from *Standing Female Nude* by Carol Ann Duffy. Published by Anvil Press Poetry, 1985. Copyright © Carol Ann Duffy.
Reproduced by permission of the author c/o Rogers, Coleridge & White Ltd., 20 Powis Mews, London W11 1JN.
Imtiaz Dharker *'Tissue'* used with permission from Bloodaxe Books, on behalf of the author. www.bloodaxebooks.com.
Carol Rumens *'The Emigree'* used with permission from Bloodaxe Books, on behalf of the author. www.bloodaxebooks.com.
Beatrice Garland *Kamikaze* from *The Invention of Fireworks* by permission of Templar Poetry
Checking Out Me History copyright © John Agard 1996 reproduced by kind permission of John Agard c/o Caroline Sheldon Literary Agency Ltd.
The AQA name is used by permission of AQA.

Every effort has been made to contact all copyright holders and obtain permissions; if any copyright holder would like us to make any alterations to the acknowledgements, we will be happy to do so at the first opportunity.